WHISPERS IN THE DARK

Donald McLeod

STONE BUDDHA BOOKS

Acknowledgments

Grateful acknowledgment is made to the editors of the following publications in which some of these poems first appeared:

Tsunami, Poultry Magazine, Flow Magazine, Slipstream, Voices International, Vol. No. Magazine, Protea Literary Journal, Gas Magazine, Minotaur, Pearl, SeaTales, LedgePoetry Forum, Atheist Journal, Poetry LA, Modern Haiku, Frogpond and the author's haiku book *Small Town, Big City (All Night Press)*

Copyright © Donald McLeod

Printed in the United States of America

First Printing - 2016

Stone Buddha Books

Los Angeles, CA

ISBN-13:978-0997954302 (Stone Buddha Books)
ISBN-10:0997954302

WHISPERS IN THE DARK

CONTENTS

Whispers in the Dark 1

ALMOST TRUE CONFESSIONS
Gorilla Compound 7
The Circumvented Center 8
Action 9
The Offer 12
4 A.M. 14
Deconstructing with Tom 15
Poetry Competition 17
Wiener Roast 19
Erotic Haiku Sequence 21

PONDERINGS
A Penny for Thought 27
Means of Traversing 29
Looking for the Right Place 30
The Silence 33
Left His Mark 34
Missed Opportunities 35
Sunbathing With Dog 36
Idleness 38
April Fools 40
Infinity 42

RANTS & ROARS
The WatchTower Couple
    Come to Save My Soul 47
The Sporting Life 49
Night Sweats 50

Add Coolant 51
Pigs 53
This One's for the Shy Girl 55
The Semantics of Mime 58
Sybil, the Sequel 60
Guilty as Charged 64
Unsatisfactory Ending 65

STRANGE ENCOUNTERS
Wine Tasting 69
Woke up Wearing Dad's Head 71
How the Seamen Came to Eat Their Words 74
Cheap Motel 77
Visions of a False Messiah 78
Milk 80
Dada Baby 82
Drowning Pool 84
Dreaming of Icarus 86
Art Film 88

PERIPHERAL OBSERVATIONS
Simple House 91
Barnyard 92
Completely Bovine 93
On the "B" Circuit 95
Sand Dunes 97
The Critic Responds 98
Inside the Day 100
Morning Symphony 101
And the Tide Takes All 102
My Father Never Said Much 104
Figures 108

INTRODUCTION

The poems in this collection were written over a period of 29 years, dating from 1987 to 2016. Most were written in free verse, as I prefer to have the content dictate the form, and although I've written in established forms, I've found an open style, which the poet Robert Hass has called Leaping Poetry, was best suited to my somewhat undisciplined mind. A technique where one idea or image "leaps" to the next in an organic way.

To me a good poem is an invitation to the reader to participate in the event, provided that the poet gives them the tools to let the imagination flow. Image, sound and environment are all open to the reader's own interpretation. I have always preferred reading good poetry to movies, because in film you are largely controlled by the filmmaker's vision. He/she gives the viewer everything — visuals, sound, and story, so the viewer for the most part is a passive recipient and only needs to watch. The experience is pre-determined on every level. Whereas with poetry, the reader is invited to use the imagery created through words, to then create their own experience using language in combination with their own intelligence and creative visualization to make the poem come alive. I try to make my poetry just such an experience for the reader – so the challenge is to create word pictures that are accessible to each person's unique response mechanism, which in turn allows the reader to be a co-creator in the event.

One of my acquaintances said, "I don't read poetry – I guess because they made me read it in high school, and I don't like all that rhyming stuff. But I like your stuff – it doesn't sound like poetry. It's more like someone talking some really interesting babble." I'll take that. With luck I've found my audience.

                                                        Donald McLeod

WHISPERS IN THE DARK

"Be ready to hear what whispers in your ear"
Steven Spielberg

I hear them almost every night –
fluttering half-thoughts
vying for my drifting attention
like so many moths
wanting not wanting
the dim lightbulb of my night brain

sometimes it seems
a separate knowing entity
is in my head
twirling me towards
a cognizant message –
but then again
these faint fragments
seem to come from beyond
somewhere out in the void
that contains the me
that can never be found

voices spewed out from some
mysterious cauldron
of collective purpose
and often these whispers
dance and flit like
tap-dancing thingless things
on my skull screen
all trying to
deliver a hazy inter-woven
series of signals

both prophetic and nonsensical
such as: the self does not exist –

you are only a collection of concepts
or the Pope bowling with a severed head
or sometimes just pixilated scenes
filtered through the wordless
cover of consciousness

my long dead mother
moving her lips without words
pieces of language forming and
dissolving into word-play like

worm dust river's edge or
love fiber trench-coat then
seemingly from the depths
of memory an ex-lover
whispers I have to go now
little voices from the over-self
I can never quite become
acquainted with ... they echo
into the dark realm of near sleep
and flutter back into blankness

the daily swarm of life's moments
dissipated into jumbled shards
of word and fractured image
night whispers seeping through
the thick blackout curtains
with mad crazy visions like
a sumo wrestler sharpening a pencil
or my first grade teacher
standing on an apple
then "go to Tibet – buy a new laptop –
drink some whiskey and be somebody"

Alas ... poor Yorick has even made
an appearance ... rolling his own
blanched skull about in his long

skeleton fingers and gazing back at
the space where Hamlet ought to be
Murmured voices swirling
into nothingness like
a Salt Buddha dropped
into the sea to become one
with its ultimate source

and with a bit of luck
I drift into the warm perfection
of a deep thoughtless sleep

ALMOST TRUE CONFESSIONS

GORILLA COMPOUND

He is looking somewhere beyond us.
Beyond the space and time in
which he is contained. In his gaze
he seems to see something he can't
quite remember. Perhaps it is a
vision of his mate carrying her
young on her back as they scrambled
away from the poachers, or
a fleeting recollection of
the bitter taste of bamboo shoots,
so lush and moist upon his
massive primordial tongue.
For a second he looks through me,
as if I were a familiar painting
he'd grown accustomed to viewing,
as if I were part of a mirage
he might once have run to and found
to be empty, a mere shape on his
repetitive vista of containment.
Like a giant stoic Buddha, he blinks
once and shifts his massive head
to stare off with blank acceptance at the
phenomenon of the outside world.

THE CIRCUMVENTED CENTER

I've decided to start this poem at the end
and thus spare the reader the part about
my dear sweet dad who shambled down
the hallway in his T-shirt, went butt-naked

and shivering into the bathroom for a long
midnight pee that night before he died –
and me, just laying there in bed with an
army man stuck to my leg and a head-full

of hazy concepts I'd dreamt up like an
Ashberry poem I didn't yet know about,
while mom lay asleep in the kitchen of
her mind baking egg and potato buns and

worrying if the well might go dry before
it's off to school-up the first graders on
matters of Dick & Jane. That's the part
you missed me telling you about, which

reminds me of an editor who hates poems
about poetry and rightly so I suppose . . .
now if I were a true surrealist, I'd jump
overboard, maybe swim awhile in the wake

of old Hart Crane, take a deep bubbly dive
for the dark side, tear open my seaweed shirt
and show you Rosie on my chest. And they all
lived unhappily ever-after in a gingerbread

house on a hill like you'd find in an old
Hammer film with Oliver Reed all liquored
up and puffy-eyed and acting up a storm.
So it's about missing the middle, the
circumvented center of this that I'm getting at . . .

ACTION

I'm sitting in my gorilla suit
on a half-apple box
on the set of Naked Gun 2 1/2.
I'm sweating like a sumo wrestler
in an Osaka steam bath
while I wait for the director
to line up the wild animals
for the big escape scene –
the one where Leslie Nielsen
busts through the wall in a tank,
and all the agented zoo creatures
come charging out after him.

I'm performing as the gorilla
because I wanted to be
or not to be a Shakespearean actor
so I took a pantomime class
and the theater girls liked the part
where I made something
out of nothing and I decided
I didn't need to wear tights
or remember someone else's dialogue
and I did a great gorilla improv
and now I'm squatting here
thinking about pretty Percilla Presley
alone in her trailer
and I'm beginning to understand
how Elvis got so choked up
over those cheeseburgers
when the animal trainer yells
 "When I give the signal
you better move your ass,
cause them elephants ain't stoppin'
for nobody and they're gonna'
be right behind you!"

And at this very moment
I want to yank my suit off
and perform my mime piece de resistance
which has moved audiences to tears
and I want to show him

my volumes of poems and stories
and remind him in no uncertain terms
that I ain't some illiterate primate
but I think better of it
and just nod my sloped ape head
and resign myself to the situation
at hand which means
I may be a literate guy
in an ape suit getting SAG scale
but I'm still about to be trampled
by a herd of elephants so I hunker down
for that desperate knuckle scamper,
which could save my life
if not the film
and for no apparent reason
I suddenly think
of a Jackson Pollack painting
I'd seen in an art book
and I ponder which image is more real –
the splatters of paint in my minds eye
or the trunk-swaying elephants with their
backup posse of baboon, giraffe, llama
and this covey of squawking exotic birds –
all wild-eyed and anxious
to rush out for what they think
may be a great escape.
Then I glance over my shoulder
at the trainer, who is frantically
pointing at me and the animals
and he gives me a wild cut throat gesture

and the director bellows
    "ACTION"
I can feel the ground shaking
under the charging elephant's weight
and I'm off zig-zagging in a frantic
knuckle run for my life as a giant
ostrich flaps past me and I briefly
wonder what would have happened
had I continued with Shakespeare
and I picture with deep pleasure
all the mournful faces
of my friends and family
weeping over the tragic headline:
**GORILLA ACTOR TRAMPLED TO DEATH
ON THE UNIVERSAL STUDIOS BACKLOT**

THE OFFER

an oily little man
from the traveling sideshow
wants me to join up as
Kongo the Killer Gorilla
captured at great expense
and hauled around the world
for the fair crowd to see
for the modest sum of 75 cents
and all I gotta do is
spend seven hours a day
in my 50-pound monkey suit
inside a bamboo cage
inside an aluminum trailer
in exchange for top-billing
and $650 a week plus a cut
of the gate after five
if I just sit and stare
and pretend to be a wild and
dangerous beast who struggles
against his chains and snarls
at the gullible families
as they traipse single file
through my fern-lined grotto
to the sounds of a phony
gorilla growling out
scheduled primitive laments
on a scratchy tape with
an electric fan and free
mileage between small towns
that shut down at dusk
while I flirt with
the Rubber Lady from Toledo
to the roar of a tractor pull
and long for my home

as the dead whale exhibit
folds up for the night
and the tattooed boys roll joints
in the shadow of a dirty tent
beneath the Globe of Death

4 A.M.

Two young cops
on the Hollywood night patrol
pull up beside my steamy car.
My date and I unravel blinking
into a shaft of serious light.
The cops question my sobriety
and demand a demonstration.
I'm ripped to the gills
on sake and Sapporo dry.
But I'm also a circus performer
an acrobatic wire-walker
who doubles as Rubber Man
in an off-season sideshow.
So I spring from the car
walk the line on my hands
back-flip onto the hood
for a one-armed handstand
and then cartwheel down to
land in arabesque at their feet.
With my eyes tightly shut
I flip my top hat on my head
propeller-spin my arms around,
and intermittently touch my nose
with the tip of each finger.
The cops are genuinely impressed
and wave me away with a head shake.
I blow my date a goodnight kiss –
hop back into my funny car,
and hurtle bleary-eyed down Franklin
headed for the freeway.

DECONSTRUCTING WITH TOM

sitting at the bar
after the poetry reading
he said it was good
but none of this matters
I said an ancient zen text
says if you meet the Buddha
on the path – push him aside
he said that doesn't matter either
I said yes nothing matters
let's just make some funny sounds
he lit a cigarette
I poured my water on it
he rolled his eyes
no one said anything for awhile
I said old pond
frog waiting to jump in
does that tatter?
he said no, frogs don't wait
they either jump or not
I said old pond
frog about to jump in
because the fox approaches
that matters to the frog
but not to me he said,
about to light another cigarette
I took away his lighter
Don, he said go to dental school
move to Pocatello
marry a sweet fat girl
procreate – that matters
I lit up one of his cigarettes
someone broke a glass
in the back of the bar
we smoked in silence

then I said you know
Basho said if you write
only one good haiku
in a lifetime you should
consider ourself lucky
Tom said that's not bad ...
but the only true haiku
is found in answer to the question
what is the capital of South Dakota?
and the haiku answer is
either Pierre or I don't know
I put out my cigarette
and we both ordered
another stiff residual drink

POETRY COMPETITION

This one has all the markings of a grand-prize winner,
what with those bits of wisteria dangling like loneliness
and those meditative frogs staring wide-eyed at the
lotus pond which mirrors a white cloud drifting

through the place where they will maybe jump into like
amateur sky-divers with their appendages splayed from the
fists of their Buddha bodies. But on second thought I see
the judge is an ex-Green Beret, held captive in Nam,

where he stayed alive on a diet of insects and rice.
So maybe I'll send him the one with that pin-up girl
draped over a Chevrolet with her golden hair tossed back
like a breaking wave as she strokes the curve of a shinny

hood ornament in her oh so revealing Daisy May shorts,
with her leg up, all sinewy and full of promise, in a six-inch
heel on the hard front bumper that reflects the cream of
her thigh as it rises out from the chrome like a lone pine

revealed through the mist on a Chinese landscape painting,
like a lifeboat with a motor that's raring to go overboard
for that jettisoned sailor, when suddenly I notice
there is a second judge listed, who runs a martial-arts camp

for women of the storm. So I figure I'll pull out
the pinup and go for a name change, maybe call myself
Kitty Carlisle or Agnes de Warhead – better send in
the one about me and Alice B. Toklas having a barbecue

on Martha's Vineyard – how we stuck pins in a Teddy
Kennedy doll and then sat back in agony watching
those sailboats bobbing on Nantucket Sound till
the sun went down and so did she as we drowned

in the overbearing essence of it all – yeah
that's what I'm going to send him ... yeah.

WIENER ROAST

It was flesh that made me bold
that summer I saw her standing
like a siren in the flickering
shadows of my birthday barbecue.
Forced by the curdling nature
of hospitality, I turned away
to reflect on her position,
as well-wishers eddied towards me
bearing cards and clever gifts
to honor my good humored endurance.
I kissed cheeks and pumped hands
and zeroed in on her curvaceous
detail as she listened attentively
to her animated companion waxing
on the dualities of corporate law.

Heady with romantic appetite,
I selected a plump raw wiener
and with bun in hand I proceeded
to approach this well-kept goddess
of the para-legal underworld.
But when I asked about her future,
she just sighed and looked wistfully
back at her well-adjusted pettifogger,
who was poking his patty on the grill.
"We're planning to get married in the Fall,"
she cooed with a triumphant toss of her
long fluid hair – so I slipped
into the chattering house where
my ex-fiance and her husband
were waiting to leave, and I heaped up
a chip-load of bean dip and sat
down to watch my neighbor's wife
gesticulating with a carrot stick

on the failure of script readers
to perceive her readily available meaning
as the stereo pumped out
Ain't No Mountain High Enough
and my gums began to tighten
over the roots of my clenched teeth.

EROTIC HAIKU SEQUENCE

small restaurant
stranger's soft hair
brushes my sleeve

scent rising from
the steaming clam bowl
her come-to-me smile

depth of the universe
reflected in her eyes —
we speak of the weather

out in the field
her tousled hair
blowing with the wheat

canopy of stars
flickering in cadence
to the cricket's song

moon thru the branches
our late night stroll
becomes an embrace

she touches my wrist
telling me
she lives with someone

beneath the big sky
she cups her full breasts
to the crescent moon

her slender fingers
rippling lake water –
reeds into mist

storm clouds approaching
black stallion standing still
in the wind-blown wheat field

ascending the stairs –
the slope of her legs
slips into her skirt

lightning
my wooden hairbrush
crackling thru her hair

summer moth
wanting not wanting
the porch lightbulb

her lips take me
her dangling earrings
tingle my thigh

a night bird calls –
the breeze rustling leaves
in the yard

eating fresh plums
in the moonlight
I taste her secrets

deep inside her
a bead of sweat rolls
into her navel

sunrise
our coupled window image
fading into a flower garden

her nude shadow
fleeting and deep
behind the lace curtain

after she's gone –
a leaf falls
into her footprint

PONDERINGS

A PENNY FOR THOUGHT

I sit motionless
in a rented sedan
watching the silent winter
fall on the empty street.
A wet brown leaf
tumbles like a memory
down the cold sidewalk.
Across the street
a wind-bent and hatless
old man waits
for the light to change.
His tattered trousers
flapping like surrender flags
against his frail legs.
Braced against a mail box,
he carefully lowers himself
onto the pavement.
He is halfway across
when a honking bread truck
narrowly misses him.
The old man studies
the truck for a moment
and then plods across
to the other side.
He pauses to wipe
the rain from his brow,
adjusts his ragged coat,
and with short choppy steps
he sets off up the street.
After a few yards
he stops and peers
down at the sidewalk.
with great effort
he bends to one knee

and picks up
a wet brown penny.
He examines the coin
as if it were a jewel,
and carefully puts it in his pocket.
A heavy rain begins to fall
as the old man turns back
and wanders towards the crosswalk.
I start the car up
and pull away from the curb.
The importance of this event
will remain undeterminable.

MEANS OF TRAVERSING

To get it all going
I like to rise up and move
maybe start out with a slow shuffle
listening to the rasp of my slippers
as they slide over the spilled grit
from the kitty litter box
just choo choo chooing along
like a steam train
pulling out sure and slow
from the waving station
with a jazz band jamming
Coltrane on my platform car
till I pick up speed
and blast my horn
and groove out of control
into the wide-open spaces
of the great unknown

LOOKING FOR THE RIGHT PLACE
(for Richard Weekley)

Foggy San Francisco night
I'm alone and wandering
through North Beach
looking for culture
and the City Lights Bookstore.
Lured by the aroma
of real Italian pasta
and a few good lines
I pass invisible
through a gang squabble
past the strip joints
and street hustlers
up and down Columbus
to the slanted entrance
caught like a wedge
on the famous hill.
Sleeping Beatitude Place
that spawned Kerouac and Ginsberg
Corso and Ferlinghetti.
My leather jacket squeaks
as I push open
the heavy glass door —
desk clerk with a buzz cut
and Lennon glasses
is praising a neo-punk band
called the Idiots —
I glide past a rack
of feminist literature
and creak down the grooved steps
to the paperback basement.
Lovers arguing over
an AIDS book
local poet tacking

his reading notice above
a row of macrobiotic diet books.
Glancing up I see
a ray of light ...
could it be dear old Jack
hovering just above
the travel section?
I thumb through
Zen Driving
wanting to become
one with the road.

*You're not in the traffic
you are the traffic*

Drifting upstairs
being the climb –
big sloppy drunk bursts in
cursing and muttering
mammary accolades
in memory of
the Great Carol Doda.
Heady with language
I touch-browse down
to examine a dusty row
of small-press spines.
Knee-deep in the w's
still without a take-home
when a good friend's book
Small Diligences
catches my twisted glance.
I dust off the only copy
pass a bit of currency
and step out into misty neon night.
Over Cannelloni and red wine
I flip to a page
read a random line

You roam like you've lost
something of great value
looking in unlikely places
You negotiate with yourself
to make it through the hour

I feel comforted by
my friend's acute perceptions
of the perpetually changing
here and now
and I realize at last
I'm in the right place

THE SILENCE

just below the surface
          of a still pond
between thunder
          and lightning
between the notes
          of music
like a swallow
          in the air
or in your throat
          something felt
but not heard
          like mist
creeping
          across
a Chinese landscape
          painting
or the silence of
          an antique locket
the tick
          before the talk
a foreign language
          written in braille
the cymbal
          before the crash
gravestones
          valleys
sleeping villages
          deaf mutes
and watches
          of the dead
all roaring
          with silence

LEFT HIS MARK

with a jar full of pens
big blood-red lines
slashed through the Bible
asterisks and arrows
attacking Time and The Nation
haiku on dollar bills
and parking tickets
and his signature scrawled
on guest books
from Bombay to Boston
questioning comments
on Emerson, Jung and Thoreau
calendar days filled
with his boxed impressions
snappy summations
neatly noted on every
story, book, and poem
he ever read
even wrote his own epitaph
a week before he died
he was my best friend
but I'll be damned
if I can ever remember
him sending me a letter

MISSED OPPORTUNITIES

Sunrise
Drawing color to the trees
And me still thinking of her
Dancing beyond my reach
As though she were a rainbow
Leaping over a horizon
I could never quite touch
Lithe and sensual in form
Yet street-wise and tough
Like a scrawl of ghetto-graffiti
No you don't mess with her
But I can't help thinking
We could've had a good time
Dodging the serious world
If only we had tried to
Strip away the walls
Of calculated indifference
Which bound us into ourselves

SUNBATHING WITH DOG

lying out here
in this bare yard
sunbathing with dog
and a new book of poems

in the midst
of a no-work weekday
and the book is filled
with myth and remembrance
with longing and regret

the pale patches of grass
are buzzing with flies
and the determined chirp
of an average sparrow

beneath the plastic grid work
of my sun-dried lawn chair
a widening web
of nocturnal crawlers

is stirred to attention
by the coming flow of dusk
and the promise of a single
micro-sip of glistening dew

the roof's cool shadow
slowly takes my ankles
and the phone machine
picks up another uninspired call

dog gets up
and smells the book
in an instant
all its meaning is revealed

IDLENESS

I passed the day today in luxurious idleness
a state of inactivity I've perfected not unlike
those wizened zen masters who sat so still
that birds took to their hair and as legend has it

their legs rotted off on the road to enlightenment
and one would suppose they eventually toppled
over with necessity like so many bowling pins
being stood on their heads yes it all began with

a stiff shuffle into the john where the crooked
pee-stream splashed me into scratching my ass
and wandering into the kitchen for a gulp of
pink lemonade while the coffee brewed and the

post-modem poets in Russia lost their inertia
then I read some theory on the visual texts
of William Carlos Williams – told the meowing cat
to hold its horses while I tried to birth a poem

then staggered out into the noon day glow
to pick up the morning paper which I tossed
unopened in the big blue recycling bin
I marveled at the cracks in my bare lawn

thought about paying my back taxes
and the drudgery of ants in my planter
then went back inside to vacuum cat hair
off my counter top – got a call to pose

in my ape suit for a Tarzan convention
sent an e-mail to a nasty girl residing in Bangkok
blew my nose twice and looked out the window
to see if the possums had eaten their food
remembered a party I'd missed once again

and read the cast list of a play flyer I'd
received from someone I didn't remember
thought about ways to change the world

and settled on tweezing my nose hairs
then grabbed a couple of zen books
and travelled back into the bathroom
for a long lazy shit ... after that the day
was pretty much down hill all the way

APRIL FOOLS

on this day
I fooled no one
but myself
as often is the case
in a confessional mood
which may render
this piece disposable
as yesterday's newspaper
if I believe
what Mary Oliver said
in Blue Pastures
that I'm more catharsis
than art
more memoir than poem
but I imagine myself
more flawed than nature
more natural than man
although I'm certain
it would be fine
to just be a rabbit
or an old top hat
but back to the fool
wasn't he the one
who saved his own neck
by telling a tale
in somersaults
the king wanted to hear
so there you have it
the king and I
and Mary Oliver
all on my mind
and me
so completely at ease
without the Pulitzer Prize
as the dawn breaks

with the crow's squawk
and the jester's bell
on my nightcap
tinkles me out
of the poem and
into the quick of it all

INFINITY

This eternal concept
is devastating to comprehend.
Beyond the farthest reach of
distance and possibility ...
Or is there perhaps some
essence at the edge of infinity
which makes for an ending –
but if that were so
the nothing beyond the edge
would still have to be something
even if it were void
of time and space and matter
as we know it.
Perhaps this is where
the conceptual God of religion resides.
Some absolute pure absence,
which is manifested
as all encompassing presence –
some unmitigated blankness
beyond yet contained
in the timeless birth and death
of all phenomenal things.

As a child
I would often delight
in aggravating myself
to the point of exhaustion
over the concept of infinity.
I would thrash about in my bed,
long after my rational parents
had drifted into a deep
and natural sleep,
and say to myself
over and over

how could there be no end
something always beyond
the most distant point imaginable?
No ending at all
just unbearable continuation ...
and I would switch on my flashlight,
and take comfort in the concreteness
of my plastic G.I. Joe as he
slaughtered the comic book bad guys.
and once again rejuvenate
my belief in blessed termination.

RANTS & ROARS

THE WATCHTOWER COUPLE
COME TO SAVE MY SOUL

The Watchtower couple
came sliding right through
my spiked-iron gate
with their hopeful pious faces
and a satchel full of redemption,
they were just aching to
ram down my throat.
But since diversion
was one of my specialties,
I parried their saccharine advances
by offering them discounted copies
of my self-published haiku.
And when they refused,
I released my atheist Cockapoo,
who shot out the door at them
like he was the devil himself.

Well, I can tell you
this ham-headed pamphlet thumper
and his mousey little wife
went backing straight into a rose bush.
They howled and waved their Watchtowers
at my nasty-tempered mutt,
who growled and snapped
and leapt up and down
like a demon on a trampoline
as he tore away the pages
with his jagged razor teeth.

And when I figured they'd run
out of prophecies,
I called the beast off —
but my zen robe fell open

exposing my devilish toy,
which sent the witnesses running
straight for the pearly gates.
With my soul still intact,
I bent gently down to pick up
the shredded pieces of the Watchtower
which lay strewn on the sidewalk
like so many Japanese plum blossoms
after a hard spring rain.

THE SPORTING LIFE

did you know
old circus lions and bears
are often sold to hunting resorts
so some pathetic
slope-headed redneck
or his dude-ranch city folk kin
can kill
for the sheer pleasure of it
pop pop pop
goes the high-powered rifle
with the telescopic insight
and the old crippled lion
buckles at the shoulder rolls forward
losing his balance
losing his life
as he tumbles
without dignity
onto the hard
Texas range
and the hunter is triumphant
with his big gun and his big ego
while the grainy video souvenir shot
pans back and forth
from the man
to the beast
where it ends
and this is how
the West is fun
Christians and lions
Christians and lions

NIGHT SWEATS

It starts out
to be a small thing remembered
like a bug stepped on twenty years ago
or the way the waiter smiled last night
when I said nice tie
then it begins to bend
like the arched back of a startled cat
but remaining slight – maybe someone
sewing a severed ear
back on the door mouse
or a pin cushion
made from a goiter
on your grandmother's neck –
just small stuff
but aggravating all the same
like golfers teeing off
with a bucket of eyeballs
or the wide-eyed harpist peering out
through her strings at a prison concert
something like that.

ADD COOLANT – CIRCA 1985

I'm cruising down Ventura
in my lime-green Impala
when the warning light starts flashing
Add Coolant – Add Coolant
so I whip into 7-Eleven
for a deck of Marlboros
and some mirrored sunglasses
but the light keeps on flashing
Add Coolant – Add Coolant
so I hit up the Galleria
for some black leather pants
and a purple fedora
but the light goes right on flashing
Add Coolant – Add Coolant
so I skid to a stop
at the old Tower Records
where I buy up some tapes
by the Hooters and Blasters
and just to be sure
I dash into Aahs
for a day-glow Godzilla
and a Jimmy Dean phone
but the light is still bleeping
Add Coolant – Add Coolant
so I dye my hair blue
and moonwalk into
the video store to get
The Terminator and
Gone with The Wind
and then just to be safe
I sneak into B. Dalton
and shoplift a Bukowski
Two Sartres and a Proust
and on the way out
a friend sells me coke

in a pot with some glue
and sure enough
Add coolant – Add coolant
then I get this idea
and I head to the Shell station
where I brandish my Visa
and purchase to own a big
yellow gallon of cooling
Prestone
Add Coolant – Add Coolant
so I press down and
pull up and rupture the seal
and hey you know what
this stuff tastes pretty smooth –
kinda like warm lemon Jello ...
and the flashing light
gets
real fuzzy and
fades
outa sight

PIGS

pigs
big blunt pigs
greased and squealing
over cotton candy and wrappers
are fair game
for red-necked hog-tying brutes
stuffed pink pigs
puffed softer than babies
worn out as hats
and shaped into
slippers and bacon
that sweet long slab
of friendly sizzle
we shove sideways
into our twisted mouths
as we read the morning paper
over coffee at Denny's
we are pigs
becoming the eaten myth
that begins with a widening
of the buttocks and nostrils
and a tight protruding lump
twisting outward from the coccyx
these new shapes are drawn
from the narrowing mind
and often end upside-down
hung by the legs
from the back of a tractor
with the pink throats slit
while a rubberized man
hoses us squeaky-clean
and shovels our fat guts
into a galvanized bucket
to make room for the next lot
to be pressed into bite-sized bits

of pig parts and beans
the pigness expertly removed
like the holocaust dead and
transformed into that clinical product
we like to call pork
even ham is a soft word
safe enough for a sandwich
wrapped in plastic to be eaten
by nursery school children
so far removed from the
oinking hoary boxcars
guarded by sleepy-paunched men
with apples in their mouths

This One's for the Shy Girl
(at the bank-sponsored poetry reading)

This one's for the shy girl
cowered in the corner with her
page full of trembling words
that flutter and stick to her
dry lips – when all she has
to know is that we do want
to care, despite our founded
concern over breath mints
and the exact time of day.

This one's for the girl
with no name and a rumpled
skirt folded like hens' wings
over her worn blue shoes.
She is a natural and necessary
antithesis for the vindictive
fur-lined felines strutting
down Sunset headed for Rodeo
with their over-budgeted
boyfriends and that rectangular
slice of plastic, which always
stays hard and neatly tucked
within the scaly walls
of their snake-skin purses.

Yes, you have come to the right
place tonight to hear the
dip and sway of cool vowels
warbled from the moist tongue
of a not-so-dry man, who must
hurry to complete the sentence
before the sensors learn
he's surrounded by all this poetry.

This one's for the girl
weighted with self doubt, as she
shuffles toward the podium to
exorcise the shapeless demons
who crowd the tattered edges
of her loose-leaf notebook.

Her faint words will echo
from the cold bare walls
of this bankable reading room,
and tomorrow when the talk
returns again to high fiance,
satisfaction will be measured
mathematically by an unfathomable
web of interlocked digits
and the sounds she whispered
will silently slip from
the stuccoed chinks of concrete,
where they will seep
into the agitated pores
of a fidgeting bank president,
who will pass the day uneasy
and later that night
will dream a sweaty montage
of nickel-plated lizards
playing poker with his holdings
while an extinct blue whale
blows soap-bubble riddles
from a liquid tapestry.

He will awake with an alarming
desire to allocate funds
for the unconditional support
of the small-press publishers,
and a feverish need to rewrite
the Wall Street Journal
in iambic pentameter.

And during breakfast
he will actually taste
his microwaved waffles
as he scribbles free-verse notations
on his monogrammed tie.
And when he reaches the office,
he will back out of a take-over,
before hurrying off to be enlightened
by a wigwam wizard
smoking a strange pipe
and reading Gary Snyder poems
in the wavering moonlight.

THE SEMANTICS OF MIME

mime (mim) mimed, miming
the art or technique
of portraying
a character, mood, idea
or narration by gestures
and bodily movements
2. a performer
  specializing
  in this art

Marcel Marceau
Etienne Decroux
(the founding father of modern mime)
Jean-Louis Barrault
      from
Chaplin, Keaton and Harold Lloyd
      mime
once associated with
fantastic illusion
high culture
poetic kinetic silence
      poignant gesture crystalized
movement
artistic purity
pure mime dying

now mime a cliche to itself
killed by
television and commercials
where cutesy kissing mimes
appear on cue
as striped mobil props
to support and promote
some commercial enterprise

mime killed by
eager sloppy white-faced youth
on street corners
in shopping malls
miming
empty imaginary walls
and irritating the public
for a dollar
charm
is not a forced characteristic
but an extension of truthfulness
if we allow
the clarity of gesture
to die man will be lessened
in body and eventually in mind
swallowed by his own
technological advancement
The mime
must find his soul again
and step bravely out
with censorious eye
and "speak" to the heart of the heart
of humanity
new mime
a thoughtful and skilled practitioner
of soulful gesture
a wise and entertaining interpreter
of life all around us

SYBIL, THE SEQUEL

She is blonde and beautiful
and very dangerous.
She has the kind of body
that could make a priest
kick a hole in the confessional.
She appears to have it all together
in her tight skirt and spiked heels,
which could puncture a lung
if she ever caught you
in a compromising position.
We're out having dinner,
when for no apparent reason
she turns into Sybil,
the R rated sequel,
co-starring me and all the men
who ever done her wrong.
"Look at all these jerks
starring at me," she snaps,
"and their wives just hate me
'cause I'm beautiful
and everyone in this
stinking restaurant knows it!"
I'm thinking,
No, they're just curious
because your tits
are practically popping out
of your leopard-skin top,
and they're wearing belts
that are wider than that strip
of leather you call a skirt.
But being a lover of anatomy
and an amateur diplomat,
I just say,
"They're only jealous,"
which sets off some

raw and tweaked nerve
in her head, and she starts
cutting me up like
an under-paid editor
sniping outtakes
from a bad B movie
that's gone way over budget:
"you're an asshole,
and jerk-off! You're
the shortest guy I've
ever dated ..."
I cut her off with,
"Could you please pass the salt."
The normality of my request
catches her off guard,
and she hands me the shaker.
I sprinkle a few granules onto
a filleted slap of fresh red meat.
She licks her lips and says,
"You could never satisfy me
sexually – I'm into really
big guys, and she tosses
her hair back and then she
belts down another double
White Russian.

I skewer up another
stale chunk of white bread
and twirl it like a wand
through the fondue cheese-pot,
which is beginning to bubble
like the La Brea Tar pits
or the deep throated vent
of Mt. Vesuvius,
just before eruption.
And then she's off
and strutting it real slow,

between the tables
to the ladies room
for a lengthy touch-up even
Earl Shieb couldn't
fail to appreciate.
So I plank down a C note
and we're outta there —
headed for a splash down
at a neighborhood bar
with generous drinks
and a no-cover blues band,
when she starts in again.
"Nobody loves me,
they just want to boff me!
and I say,
"I like you," which ends up
sounding like bad Dick & Jane
dialogue, so she belts me
with a back hand and then
bares a swollen breast
as I dive to cover her
and then she's laughing,
and crying and grabbing
for my crotch
when an old female friend
from my married days
walks into the bar and says,
"How've you been?"
But before I can answer,
Sybil jumps down her throat
like Patton on a whimpering G.I.
and says, "If you want guys
to notice you, you should really
lighten your hair!
Nobody's gonna look at you twice,
looking like that in this town!"
Well, the friend freaks and hisses,

"You bitch," and bristles off
probably no longer wondering
how I've been, and Sybil says, "Oppsee."
And I say,
"I think you're blowing it,
blowing it in a big way,"
and she belts me again –
only this time
it's the kind of a slap
that jars your jaw like
the recoil from a rocket launcher,
and sends you hair flying
off your head
until it bounces and lands askew
on the wrong side
of your jiggling mug.

My google-eyed friends
are all starring at us
like they just swallowed their tongues,
so I say, "Let's get outta here,"
and I drag her past the blues band
who are singing
My Baby, She Wrote Me a Letter,
and we head for the car.
When the cold air hits her
she starts hugging me
and saying, "I think I
almost love you sweetie."
Next Morning
when I mention the incident,
she just shrugs and says,
"I guess my PMS was a little
worse than usual – call me!"
and she shoots out the door
to another Hollywood interview,
somewhere way down on Sunset.

GUILTY AS CHARGED

Along came Mary is an association
I'd rather not make, but when she showed up
I figured it was curtains and I drew them,
then the next thing I knew I was working for Disney
knocking off cartoon epics and stealing
sugar packets from the commissary
when the phone rang -
it was Reuters wanting a statement,
so I told them how I stole the cash
to get grandma a new set of jumper cables
and a one-way ticket to paradise,
but she died on the bus trip to Vegas,
so I got her a drive-thru funeral
at the Elvis Chapel
and spent what was left of the proceeds
on keno tickets and another way out
venture involving chopsticks and the I Ching,
which came up Gnawing, and I knew the time
was right for a lengthy legal process.

UNSATISFACTORY ENDING

was scribbled across my life's work.
But how could it ever be otherwise?
And what is satisfactory to the living,
that could be called an ending?
Perhaps a college campus sniping spree
ending with a quick conversion to some
serious religion before the chair is juiced,
or perhaps a life of charity and loving
brotherhood which ends with an open
casket revealing my bloodless smiling
face covered with plum blossoms
while the multitude of mourners wait
in a cold line for hours on end
to weep giant blue tears into the folds
of my rented tuxedo.

Endings are often unsatisfactory.

STRANGE ENCOUNTERS

WINE TASTING

she smiled
and deftly flicked
a bead of sweat
from the bottle's
long elegant neck
she crossed her legs
and shook her fluid
amber locks
then released the buckle
from one of her snakeskin boots
I unscrewed
the tight virgin cork
till it popped
and poured a perfect
inch-deep sample into my
Waterford crystal glass
try to use all your senses
she said with a liquid laugh

with flared nostrils
I inhaled the scent
of the pale golden nectar
once, twice, and then
a third time
just to be certain
it's a fräulein dancing
in a dewy meadow
with a slight breeze
and tiny metallic flowers
scented with a touch
of lemon bubble bath
and I think ...
two Yorkshire puppies
barking in the background

my thoughts exactly she bubbled
now taste it
but don't swallow right away
let it glide around
touching all your
hidden taste buds
and when I swallowed
the room exploded
into an enchanted vista
with prancing unicorns
and a tumbling leprechaun
but the amber-haired girl
was nowhere to be found
so I gave it an 85
and moved on
to the next bottle

WOKE UP WEARING DAD'S HEAD

the lumberous hydraulic slam
of first-light trash trucks
crashes me awake
like a hangover alarm
or a missing page
from a Sidney Sheldon novel
only that ain't the half of it
I though I heard myself say
out loud to no one
then my old man's head
settled into place
and started yammering
away like there was no tomorrow

no what you need boy
is a swift kick
in the seat of your brain
hell you ain't worth a damn
want to change the world
smack 'um around a bit
make everybody wakeup
and realize you really are somebody
too much damn zen
if you ask me
flipping spiders out the window
and watching the moon drift
between a couple of swaying palms
hell you ain't done a damn thing
in weeks 'cept drain a few dozen
beer bottles and maybe clip
your toenails on a good day
hell when I was your age
oh I am your age
yes of course I realize
I'm living alone

but what the hell gives you
the right to speak in the vernacular
when all this debate over
Shakespeare rolls on unresolved –
I'll tell you what I think
it's high time you found a rhythm
put a Dixie flag on your pickup
and kicked some ner-do-well's ass
yeah I got half a mind
to wipe that smirk
right clean off the mirror
but I suppose it never lies
so I'll just change expressions
save myself a swollen knuckle

and you can damn well bet
that old Rosicrucian
was on to something
when he told me as a kid
in college to stick a dot
on the glass and stare at it
until something happened
hell if I know what he meant
its all the same though
a line of snort, a whiff of blow
guzzling your guts full of
rot till you puke
you'd be better off
just butting your thick head
against an old tree trunk
but what the hell do I know
it's up and under 'um
ride my trike in circles
through the yard
get my ass started
on a doomsday novel
stick in some fundamentalist

crusaders who round up
them thinking folk
into a smart camp
and wear 'um down
with attrition and sermons
on Nietzsche's demise
hell I might even
have them herding hybrid
cows gone mad from milking
and grown to a good ten feet tall
have the smartie leader
escape by hiding in a uterus
after he breeds with a traitor
in a nun's habit
save the species
start a new race kinda thing ...
hell ... I don't know

HOW THE SEAMEN CAME TO EAT THEIR WORDS

In the fishmonger's kitchen
imagine a silver colander
heaped with steaming similes –
those fanciful strands
still wet and twitching,
sucked down by gravity
toward the pinhole light
till they pasta-wriggle
down and out to poke
their dangling headless
bodies through scratched tin
portholes where a ring
of red-faced seamen sit
mute and crack-lipped
around a table
made from fishbones
whose departed tissue
throbs through the veins
of the minister's daughter
and undulates the tongues
of the curtain-parted villagers
as the club-footed lunatic
follows her to the wharf

The seamen
who speak only in signs
suddenly notice the similes.
They list and sway and reel
in the soggy dripping strands
onto their long wet tongues.
They swallow in unison
and look about amazed –
they have found a new language.

"The sea is like a woman,
her islands protruding like
swollen breasts beneath
the moon's aureole – and the
jewelry of fish jettisoned
from our dripping nets –
save one, a mermaid we kept
who strangely resembled
the minister's daughter,
as she cooed to us in bubbles."

The heavy-clothed lunatic
runs pell-mell down the pier
to greet the tiny skiff
as it drifts through the
mist with its silent
curvaceous catch lying limp
and shinning in the swirls
and twists of brindled seaweed.
The villagers swarm the shoreline
to hear the seamen's tale.
"It was like being tossed about
in a huge caldron
by the angry breath of Neptune,"
says the first mate.
"Nay, ya bloody fool," says another,
"it was as if we were minnows
in the churning belly
of a venomous retching sea-monster!"
And a third interrupts –
"We was like spiders on a leaf,
racing down a cobblestone gutter
durin' a torrential downpour –
an' by Christ, lemme tell ya
somethin' else – the way that
goddam mermaid jus sat thar
blinking her moon eyes at me,

like she was some kinda
wounded doe, well, it was
enough ta break my bleedin' hart.
But we had ta keep her ya know."

The fishmonger cackles to herself,
and hurries home to hatch
another batch of words –
enough to feed the entire village,
and soon everyone is likening
one thing to another
as they gather in gleeful groups
to feverishly distort the truth,
while the lunatic paces
the pier clutching a handful
of mermaid-hair and mumbling,
"It was language that made me do it!"

CHEAP MOTEL

Cheap motel
steeped in the scent
of discount ammonia
and that lingering vision
of a kinky black hair
the size of a bobby pin
that lies like a question mark
at the base of the john.
Cheap motel
with mysterious stains
and snore-thru walls
that keep you contained
from the dangerous sounds
of a sidewalk dispute
and the thundering rumble
of a midnight freight train
that almost masks
the insatiable sounds
of the upstairs copulaters
while you stare wide-eyed
at the flickering fragments
of a bad B-movie and wonder
how many drooling psychopaths
are fondling keys to your room
while the half-moons rise
on your chewed fingernails
and the somnolent
desk clerk cracks open
another Butterfinger bar
and crumples the wrapper
into a loose ball
as she turns the yellowed page
of a paperback murder book.

VISIONS OF A FA1SE MESSIAH

A strange conical light
shafted from the forehead
of an on-rushing train
is boring dawn on you
as you stand on the tracks
petrified or resigned
as you wish.
Above on the embankment
marauding wolves
are banding together like
a Yukon wilderness painting,
when this certain light
begins to blink
egging you on
to enter
another dimension
where "egging" becomes
a fantastic vision
of smooth white ovals
with stick-pin legs
and triple-digit hands
frantically waving at you
until you dig them –
then a spiraling fall
into a dank abyss
where stalactites dangle
like the festered fingers
of a long dead corpse ...
but you drift off asleep
only to awaken cotton-mouthed
and sweating from a jagged dream,
which found you surrounded
by baskets of fish
you'd somehow been saving
for the new Centurion

sent to assist you
in matters of division,
as you stood wobbling
on that Plexiglas platform
(just below the water line)
waving your loaves
of french bread at those
blind fishermen who were
smiling toothless
through their torn nets
as they passed you by
on their way to Galilee.

MILK

A droplet of mother's milk
trickles down the infant's chin.
The yew flinches as the lamb
butts her swollen udder.
Gutters fill with foaming white liquid.
Storm clouds gather and burst,
flooding the valleys with nature's nectar.
A million purring cats run
wild-eyed to sea cliffs –
creamy-white tsunami swells
on the horizon.
A thousand miles away
at the mansion, playmates pause
to fondle their tingling breasts.
Back-bent female baboons snarl
as twin funnels of warm milk
pump into the heavenly vines above.
A great milky wave breaks
over the sleeping village.
A spinning wooden ladle bobs
past a shrinking church steeple.
Old Faithful erupts
spewing a fountain of whey
on the gaping tourists.
The tit-mouse turns
to nurse her squealing young.
IV bottles turn to white
pumping healing fluid
into flexing withered arms.
An alabaster river
flows over the dam.
Polar bears gather to lap
the sweet ivory glaciers.
Mother wipes the infant's chin
and the pearly waters recede.

From behind a cloud
the moon slips out —
its smooth reflection shimmering
on a white puddle.

DADA BABY

The baby in his crib
lies silent and wide-eyed
in a shaft of moonlight.
Overhead a mobile with ducks
is spun by a familiar
large hand.
One of the ducks begins
to honk and flap its wings.
The crib railings turn
into giant redwood trunks,
and the twirling ducks
look like stubby airplanes,
only he doesn't know this.
His pacifier tastes faintly
of soap and musk oil.
A clown on the wall
says can you say momma?
Then the door opens
and a magician enters.
He spins his cane
and it turns into a flower.
The baby finds this routine,
and soils his diaper.
A silver spoon clinks
against a glass,
or maybe it was an anvil.
A dove flies out
from the magician's nose
and the baby smiles
and thinks about nothing,
while a blue sheep
jumps through a tire
and the toilet is flushed.
In the next room
an agitated Yorki

yaks at the buzzing door,
and already the baby
is beyond remembering
what he didn't need
to understand.
Then a red ball rolls
up the bedroom wall,
and his Dankin monkey
is a soft brown thing
that just feels good.
Logos is just a word.
Everything is non-sense
and stimulation –
a phantasmagoria of nameless
sensation – the ultimate satori.
In the mother's room,
Nietzsche and Li Po
rest spine to spine,
content to collect
an ever-deepening layer
of dust and decaying
particles of the past.
Now go baby go
carpe diem
memento mori
gurgle and coo
until you Emmanuel Kant
no more,
cause it won't ever
get any better than this.
The world of language
and reason soon turns
to pablum in our pants.

THE DROWNING POOL

The neighbor boy,
the one with the translucent skin
and sad blue eyes,
was last seen yesterday
walking down to the river.

His mother described him
as small for his age,
and susceptible to flights of fancy.

Sleepy stippled trout loll like rajahs
above the emerald mossy carpet of sun-lit silt.
The truant boy is perched overhead
on the lip on a jagged rock.
He holds a smooth pebble,
which he rubs like a jewel,
between his thumb and forefinger,
as if he were drawing himself into the stone.

He releases his grip
and the pebble plummets
until it drops with a gentle plop
through the glossy skin of the water,
leaving in its wake
a widening ring of glimmering ripples.
The pebble's descent is slowed to a swirl,
as it shifts direction like a knuckleball
through the sparkling mellifluous light.
The trout flinch and scatter
to settle near the ribs of a sunken barrel.
The pebble twirls deeper and deeper
towards the jeweled depths
till it comes to rest alongside
the murky flattened form of a molted bullhead,

who twitches and flicks his thorny spine
before daring to nibble the pebble's
smooth edge with primordial curiosity.

The boy is transported into a liquid day-dream
as a thin water snake skims
the now placid surface,
severing the boy's inviting image
with its tiny thrashing tail.

DREAMING OF ICARUS

I dreamt I awoke
and found myself cuddled
next to Jane Fonda's warm thigh.
I was bruised and bleeding
and covered with seaweed!
Eunuchs were summoned
and they blew me dry
with antiseptic breath.
Jane stroked my brow
with the back of her hand.
Sunlight dripped from her
Barbarella hair and fell in
golden puddles on my chest.
She told me I was found
on the far shore whispering
Proserpina's name.
I said, "I saw her form
floating limp on the waves."
Jane nodded her head and
clapped in the slave girls –
Curtains were quickly drawn
over the bare wet walls.
I was stripped naked
and bound with Spandex.
Jane's fingers sprouted talons –
her thigh became a rock
and the eunuchs morphed
into vultures.
"My waxed wings
are floating in the sea,"
I cried "and my father's mourning
has turned to murder!"
Jane smiled knowingly, and said
"You have to work out!"
I struggled to free myself

as the primitive beat began —
rows of tight-lipped dancers
aerobicising towards me
punching the close air with
sharp fists and kicking at me,
as they bounced ever closer
while the bobbing-headed
vultures kept time to the beat
and the throbbing walls pressed
in on me until I awoke
in a cold disco sweat.

ART FILM

EXTREME CLOSE UP – Bag lady's shadow draining down a park bench
PULL BACK to reveal shorn sheep staring down at their wool
CUT TO a flock of Starlings reflected in the cow's moist eye
PAN ACROSS water ZOOM IN ON barnacles still clinging to a dead whale's belly PULL BACK to include rusted car frame half buried in sand on the Mexican beach
DISSOLVE into momentary dolphins woven in the curl of a wave
CUT TO blue glaciers
SOUND OF a finger snap ricocheting off the ice
CROSS FADE into MEDIUM SHOT of an arcing hand scattering seeds to the white chickens
SUPER IMPOSE shot of farm boy practicing his trumpet beneath a migration of geese CUT TO CLOSE UP of a horsefly buzzing in the clotheslined pantyhose
DISSOLVE to cat watching a toadstool filling with moonlight
CUT TO funeral parlor CLOSE UP of a cut lily curling into itself
SLOW FADE TO BLACK -

END CREDITS ROLL

PERIPHERAL OBSERVATIONS

SIMPLE HOUSE

We lived in a rickety old house
      about a mile from the dusty town.
Thin wooden walls bearded by fuchsia
      and covered with a Tom Sawyer white wash
that flaked to the touch.
      Loose board on the third porch step
and a litter of kittens nursing
      by the rotting woodbox.
Inside, hundred-watt light cast old-movie shadows
      on the couch-gouged linoleum.
Termite spit balls lined the windowsill
      beneath a cracked pane which reflected dad's
rhythmic fire-side rocking.
      Now and then the old collie growled at the
flourishing field mice in the attic.
      A red RCA tuber spewed war news
and the Breakfast Club – Don McNeil was
      our Johnny Carson – Richard Nixon our nemesis
and the bookmobile our savior.
      No locks on the doors and nothing steal,
except for my Dick Dale and the Deltones record
      spinning on the scratchy old Silvertone.
Mom canning plums in delicious aroma
      while the proper-named chickens lived on.
Mildewed Dickens touching wild blackberry brambles
      that grew through a crack in my bedroom wall.
Father out back in the stormy field
      fighting off the highway planning commission.
Now the old house and the loved ones are gone
      and I'm left here alone in the city
with a head-full of fading memories.

BARNYARD

the arc of mother's hand
        scattering seeds to the chickens
hens viewing each new moment
        from a different angle
rooster's blood-red comb
        wobbling over his tentative strut
pitchfork stuck in a hay bale
        screech of a circling chicken hawk
storm clouds approaching
        old mare shifting in her stall
sow bugs tightened
        under a warped board
little boy alone talking
        in the hayloft
hail roaring down
        on the rusted tin roof
a nest of pink mice
        in father's old work hat
dusty suitcase holding
        a nudie magazine
and an empty tin of Copenhagen
        sunbeam shafted through
a cloud break
        cow's tongue filling
the salt lick groove
        supper bell rings
from the glowing house
        croaking hoof prints
flashing in moonlight
        pea soup boiling
on the pot bellied stove

COMPLETELY BOVINE

the cow
contains an inherent largeness
which upon close inspection
seems utterly imploded
with the pure force of shape

emerald flies
dance in ecstasy
on the quivering flank
ready to dart back
from the thick tail swish
which flicks and twitches
with the dumb persistence
of winter wiper blades

a brittle snap –
a spurt of arced blood
the steer steps back
to stare down without recognition
at his severed horn

a flock of fleeting starlings
is reflected in the
bulging moist eye
as the cud is chewed
into a blissful blank dream

thick pink udders
are gently hand-pulled
into a squirted ping
of splattered milk splash
in the ringing tin pail
as a rush of wildly excited
felines queue up for
the intended overspill

the stall slats are slammed back
and the stiff-legged provider
stumbles piss-slipping out
the gray barn door
where she stands blinking
at both sides of the
sparkling black sky

suctioned mud oozes behind her
as she lumbers down the deep trail
to fill herself with the sound
of croaking hoof prints
and the flash of fleeing frogs
in the pre-dawn moonlight

ON THE "B" CIRCUIT

man with a tattoo
      tacking up
           a circus poster
faded yellow tent
      rises from a concrete
           parking lot
used-car salesman
      watching from a window
           his little boy smile
dusk
      midget playing solitaire
           in a rusted trailer
tape recorded fanfare
      skips
           a beat
ringmaster's
      flamboyant gestures –
           his underarm sweat rings
round and round
      the elephant's
           heavy sadness
crack of the whip
      the caged lion's
           circular pacing
handfuls of popcorn
      suspended near mouths –
           wire-walker wobbles
acrobat in a tutu
      grinds out a cigarette
           with her point shoe
clown in the dressing room
      pouring cheap vodka
           into his painted smile

a ring of trash bags
        where the tent
                used to be
semi-truck and trailer
        rumbling with tigers
                outside the coffee shop

SAND DUNES

holding the last pink wisps
of sinking sun and the
slow rushing sound
of a receding wave

a woman on horseback
appears from a sandy crest
the breeze sweeps her hair
across her tanned shoulders
as she watches the waves

I gaze at her
but my observation seems
an intrusion of the moment
and I quickly look away ...
warm sumer sand slips
through my fingers

when I look up she is gone
and I watch the tide
draw the hoof prints
into a setting memory
of a woman on horseback
looking out to sea

THE CRITIC RESPONDS

summer heat
      slowing my step
           at the wax museum

Upon careful study of the poem's first line, it would appear that it is indeed warm outside, but when viewed on a deeper psychological level, we see the poet may well mean to imply an internal rise of temperature, indicative of either subdued passion or a lingering fever held over from some recent infirmity. The brilliant juxtaposition of "heat" and "summer" can only lead one to the conclusion that the poem was set in the Western Hemisphere, unless of course the poet was indeed in Africa or some other such country, and under the delusion of the aforementioned illness – in which case we would have to assume the equatorial influences of winter would, despite the possibilities of fever, give the line an entirely different set of rules and external stimuli to act upon.

Perhaps my favorite of the lines, "slowing my step" brings us into the poet's heart and more importantly into his modes of traversal. We can almost hear the universal heart beat in the iambic fall of the stresses: slow ing' my step' ... the breathtaking imagery of a slowed step is rare in Western poetics, and again I'm reminded of Keats' "And one behind the other slepp'd serene," which contains the same surefooted means of human propulsion. A "slowed step" is so much more revealing than to just say "he stepped," for slowed is a powerful transitive verb. We're literally slowed down – invited in as it were, and given a front row seat at the linguistic cinema. On the screen of our mind we see a giant foot, held in suspended animation (perhaps, but not restricted to, a sidewalk) and our identification is nearly complete. This held sense of perpetual motion is indeed wondrous. It's as if we too were walking and suddenly felt the mystical compulsion to bring everything to a virtual standstill. This is a poet who is not afraid to take a stand – to step boldly forth and lead the way into the twenty-first century. We can only trudge behind, with heads bowed in obsequies gratitude.

The final line "at the wax museum," is with due apologies to Messrs Elliot, Pound and Williams, one of the most lucid and resonant end lines I've seen in decades. Interestingly enough, "at the" sets up the prepositional magic – it is so exact, we can sense where we are. "at the," so pregnant and full of possibility. Are we at the dump, at the store, at the university? ... No! The poet of lesser vision might easily have settled for one of these lessor locals. But our poet has dared to make the leap. He has taken us to that mysterious place locked deep in the subconscious of our muted inner child – the wax museum! And dare I be so bold as to name that city? At first I thought it was Los Angeles – but as I pondered the rhythms and internal meanings of the line, it became clear we were in my very own New York. I could "hear" the stagnant gnaw of trash rotting in a nearby basket. I could "smell" the immigrant taxis, and "see" the tinkling bell of a messenger boy, as he peddles through the stall of progress with his careless bundle of packages.

Yes, we are in New York and it is hot and our step is slowed And suddenly we recognize a bit of ourselves in the radiant thusness of this sad tattered man as he melts into the malevolent city like a wax figure in the furnace of our imagination. I will admit that upon reading that last line, I broke down and began to openly weep like a joyous school boy. Never again will I pass this great building with an air of detachment. I will lower my gaze in the summer heat and slow my step and become enraptured as I recall this magnificent poem – indelibly imprinted on the wax museum of my mind.

Dingus Fulcrum, ESQ

INSIDE THE DAY

the generous day
rolls over us
with unrehearsed certainty
it rises and falls back
bigger than wars and roses
drawing us into its folds
drawing in the still life
and the minute movements
of unseen insects
the day and all it means
pushing itself onward
to enter the past
moves without center
passes edgeless
and silent into the next

yet sometimes we must pause
to feel the moments
feel the weight of shadows
lingering over peripheral corners
pull ourselves up
into the gravity of rain
we must move like a river
always touching the same banks
with a new part of ourselves
and then step back to consider
the harmony of breath
which spirals through us
with absolute being and purpose

MORNING SYMPHONY

With the first glow of dawn
Neckless sparrows
Fidget on the frozen branch
The sun's first rays
Creep golden through
Layers of silhouetted pine
From the south
A wisp of cabin smoke
Curls into
The luminous bluing sky
Poplars and a horned stag appear
Doubling their image
On the glassy lake
A gentle mountain breeze
Breathes mist across
The far shore
From the forest depths
The flapping screech of crows
Bolts the stag
I breathe deep
And step out into
The crackling morning

AND THE TIDE TAKES ALL

night falls
like a seamless black cloak
over the secret inlet cove
a passing cloud
reveals the swollen moon
her bone-white body
lies gently extended
like a silk glove
at the lip of the sea
a ridge of light
rides the rolling swells
reaches into her pores
deepening her sculpted shadows
as she parts her trembling thighs
taking in the long cool shaft
of summer moonlight
kissed by foam
her dark cleft opens
beneath the tautly drawn
slope of her wet belly
her breasts are distended beacons
of desire sharply tipped and
brushed by the warm swirling breeze
a wave breaks curling itself
over her slender ankles
a second wave comes harder
breaks into her darkness
sucks her down
into its receding pull
again and again she is taken
by the deepening reach of the sea
a primitive surging muscle
opening her like a flower
lapping at her quivering petals

releasing forbidden juices
her nostrils flare
the quick sharp breaths
coming faster than the sea
drawing pearls of white light
from the throbbing sky
shuddering her being into
a complete release
until she blasts apart
and rolls spent on the shore
to taste the glimmering sand

MY FATHER NEVER SAID MUCH

My father never said much
wore the same floppy pants
with frayed suspenders
and a gray work shirt
for days on end.
His sweat-soaked work hat
had long since taken on the shape
of his weathered old head
and plead as mother might
he would more often than not
wear it in the house
shielding his sacred noggin
from the over-bearing
glory of Allah.

My father was all gnarl and groove
like the worn wooden pegs
holding his rocking chair
and the family together.
He had gone deaf
from exploding shells
in *World War One*
and now seemed to enjoy
the ever-clinging silence
that made our fireplace glow
with image and warmth,
while the flapping soundless lips
of mom's gossipy friends
were of no more bother
or concern to him
than an unseen covey
of morning doves scattered
by a wind-blown leaf.
In utter silence my dad

tirelessly caught my fastballs
and curves as they increased
in velocity until one day
a slider splintered his finger
and he said in plain English
I'm getting too goddamned old
to catch you and he stomped off
to rinse his wounded hand
in the cow's watering trough.

My dad never said much
just went out and got things done.
Fixed broken things and read
old dusty novels he picked out
for no apparent reason
twice a month from the bookmobile
when it rolled into town.
He always read the last chapter first
and then turned back to see
how it all had gone so wrong.
He didn't know who Jack Benny was,
never owned a television,
always figured pro baseball was "rigged"
and once punched out an umpire
for missing a third strike
with me on the pitching mound.

Only went once to the doctor
and that was because he'd passed out
and old man Ormsbee had rushed him
in the town ambulance
to the Fort Bragg hospital
some forty miles away.
When he awoke
he yanked out the EKG wires –
got me on the one-way phone
and whispered ... pick me up NOW!

Went running down the hall
with his white ass flaring out
under that half-gown said
I don't give a good goddamn
about my clothes,
just get me the hell outta here
before they kill me – hell,
Ruby could buy a damn nice dress
for what these bastards are charging.
So we drove down
the foggy coast in silence,
and five years later
he would be gone
after packing in a heavy load
of twisted driftwood
from the Anderson State Beach.
He never complained
just stacked up the wood
against the side of the house,
went to bed at eight
got up at midnight to pee
and pitched down hard
on the cold linoleum floor
where my mom found him
and wouldn't accept that he was gone
even until the day she died
six months later from loneliness
on a rainy December day in 1971

That night the dogs got out
and ran all the way into town
where they were killed
by a lumber truck
on Highway One while I drank beer
with the college crowd in San Diego
and I still can't believe
I didn't get to say goodbye

so the best I can do now
is to write this poem
as a tardy farewell
leaving these inadequate words
as a brief remembrance to the
countless silent moments
my father rarely spoke of.

FIGURES

She's thirty-five
and missing a tooth.
In a dark nightclub
under platinum hair
she looked pretty good.
He's nineteen and
built like a cedar –
had five jobs and
two years of school.
It's four a.m. and
they're sitting in
the Cake & Steak
having bacon & eggs.
He thinks she's twenty-nine.
She thinks he's twenty-five.
Next weekend she'll
lead him into a field
where she'll unfold
her portable table
and give him
a holistic message.
Two months later
he'll be working on
her father's hog farm
and by this time
next year they'll be
having a child
somewhere out west
of Decatur

About the Author

Donald McLeod's writing career began at the age of five, when he created what he calls his *Bessie Stories*. These were almost nightly reverse bedtime stories he told to his parents for a period of five years. The stories were his imagined reflections of the goings on in his small town of Greenwood, California where he grew up, and featured his imaginary "bear" friends, Bessie, Bruce, Boo, Benny and Caterpillar.

As a slightly more mature writer, McLeod has written both fiction and non-fiction, screenplays, haiku and longer poetry, much of which is found in this collection. For five years he was co-editor of the literary journal *Vol. No. Magazine*. His poetry has been published in many literary publications in North America, Europe and Japan.

McLeod has been a professional mime/movement artist for the past 46 years. He is perhaps best known for his work as the *American Tourister Gorilla* in the company's 15 year luggage campaign, and for his acting work in feature films, which include Peter Pan's Shadow in *Hook*, the gorilla in *Trading Places* and *The Man With Two Brains*,, along with his portrayal of TC the werewolf in the classic horror film *The Howling*. He lives in Los Angeles with his cat Benny, and a revolving collection of raccoons, possums, squirrels and wild birds.

www.ingramcontent.com/pod-product-compliance
Lightning Source LLC
Chambersburg PA
CBHW020012050426
42450CB00005B/426